Mega-cool Leaders

Contents

Director's Message
YUVA Books

Dear Reader,

I'm glad you picked up this book. It means you're interested in Bharat's history, which is a good start. When we think of history, we often picture a list of endless dates, wars, and the struggle to remember the chronology of the governor generals of India—enough to put anyone off! I, too, did not enjoy history as a subject in school because of how it was taught. And sadly, not much has changed in the years that have followed.

We spoke to many children about this, and we got a standard answer: History is boring. This became a challenge for us. How could we make history interesting, inspiring, and exciting? How could we go beyond the insipid details of dates, chronologies, and dynasties to give it a breath of fresh air?

Indian history, right from colonial times, has been taught with a Western worldview. It has made us feel ashamed and apologetic about our past. We have been taught that certain dynasties or empires mattered more than others. We have been fed the central-regional divide without knowing what makes some histories central or regional.

While researching for my eighth book, *Bravehearts of Bharat: Vignettes from Indian History*, I grappled with these questions. So I tried to bring into the limelight those warriors and leaders whose stories were ignored or dismissed in the past as merely regional. This was also part of the vision that guided the creation of the Foundation for Indian Historical and Cultural Research (FIHCR)—an initiative dedicated to restoring our historical and cultural legacy and fostering pride in our past.

However, research alone is not enough. History must be told in a way that resonates, especially with young minds. This is where FIHCR YUVA comes in—to make history fun, engaging, and relevant.

YUVA goes beyond textbooks to present our past through a mix of storytelling, interactive maps, documentaries, and more.

At a recent talk, someone asked me, 'What is the point of all this? Why correct or unearth history?' While the answer to that is quite long, an important part of it is that it reaches the younger generation in a language that makes sense to them and that they can relate to.

When we began the journey of FIHCR in June 2024, YUVA was perhaps the only team without a set roadmap, because we wanted to hear what young people in India had to say. And they told us that they wanted history without pressure, told in a way that sparks curiosity and pride. So, dear reader, this book is our attempt at just that. The author, publisher, illustrator, and the entire FIHCR team have worked tirelessly to bring this book to life—the one that you now hold in your hands.

It gives me great joy to introduce this remarkable book by renowned historian Dr Pradeep Chakravarthy, which brings to life the inspiring tales of five extraordinary rulers of Bharat—leaders who shaped history with their courage, wisdom, and unwavering commitment to their people. I extend my heartfelt gratitude to Pradeep for his dedication to historical storytelling and for making these narratives accessible to young readers. I sincerely hope this book inspires countless young minds to learn from the past and lead with wisdom in the future.

Happy reading!
Warm regards,
Dr Vikram Sampath
Author/Historian/Fellow of the
Royal Historical Society UK
Founder-Director, FIHCR

2000 CE
1800 CE
1600 CE
1400 CE
1200 CE
1000CE
800 CE
724 CE - 760 CE

Lalitaditya Muktapida

The Empire Builder Who Put Kashmir on the Map (r. 724–760 CE)

In the beautiful valley of Kashmir where snow-capped mountains met lush green meadows, a young prince named Lalitaditya Muktapida was born into the Karkota dynasty. From the beginning, it was clear that Lalitaditya was destined for greatness. Even as a boy, his sharp mind and insatiable curiosity set him apart.

In the royal court, while other children played, Lalitaditya would sit beside learned scholars, listening to tales of ancient kings and battles. 'Tell me, Master

---

The author wishes to record the help of Shreyanjana Bhattacharya in the research for some of the chapters.

Vishranth,' he once asked the court sage, his eyes wide with wonder, 'why do kingdoms rise and fall?'

Vishranth, a man known for his wisdom, paused before answering. 'Kingdoms rise with courage and fall with arrogance. A ruler must think of his people before himself. Remember this, young prince.'

Lalitaditya took these words to heart. His education was rigorous, combining practical lessons with a deep knowledge of governance. He mastered the art of warfare under seasoned generals, learning swordsmanship and archery. But he was equally eager to understand governance and diplomacy, often accompanying his father on matters of state.

One day, as Lalitaditya was returning from a hunting expedition, he spotted a group of farmers struggling to repair an irrigation channel. Despite his noble status, he dismounted his horse and joined them in clearing the blockage. 'A future king must know the struggles of his people,' he later told his puzzled companions.

His sense of justice burned just as brightly. Once when he saw a noble mistreating a servant, he stepped in at once. 'The strength of a kingdom,' he said firmly, 'lies in the respect its people receive.' So, even as a boy, Lalitaditya was not just learning how to rule—he was preparing to be the kind of king history would never forget.

A King Like No Other

At just twenty, Lalitaditya ascended the throne of Kashmir. His coronation was a grand affair. While the kingdom was prosperous, it was surrounded by rival powers—each waiting to test the young ruler.

On the big day, as ministers gathered in to celebrate, one elder spoke cautiously. 'Maharaja, this grand feast will display our strength to the world. It will signal that Kashmir remains unshaken.'

Lalitaditya, dressed in ceremonial armour instead of the usual silks, listened attentively. Then he said, 'And what strength will the hungry see in such feasting? While we celebrate, villages in the north are starving. Send them grain. Let the world see a king who feeds his people, not just his court.'

The court fell silent, surprised by his wisdom. It was clear that the young king cared more about his people than showing off his wealth. Determined to understand his kingdom beyond the palace walls, Lalitaditya soon

Martand Sun Temple

set out on a journey. Dressed as an ordinary traveller, he walked among farmers, craftsmen, and traders, listening to their troubles.

One evening, in a quiet village, he met an elderly weaver. 'Tell me, what troubles your heart the most?'

The old man hesitated, then sighed. 'The taxes are fair, but the officials demand bribes before helping us.'

Lalitaditya's expression hardened. 'Justice must not be sold,' he declared. Upon returning to his court, he kept a closer watch on local officials, ensuring corruption was swiftly punished.

Outsmarting Yasovarman

One of Lalitaditya's greatest victories was over King Yasovarman of Kanauj, a ruler of a vast and powerful kingdom. Kanauj controlled key trade routes and had a formidable army. But for Lalitaditya, this war was more than a conquest—it was his vision of uniting Bharat under a strong and wise leadership.

Before marching to battle, Lalitaditya called a midnight council with his commanders. 'Yasovarman's strength lies in his numbers and his pride,' he said. 'But pride often blinds. He expects us to attack his capital, so we will strike where he least expects—his supplies and allies.'

The army moved swiftly, cutting off Kanauj's lifelines and turning Yasovarman's allies against him! Furious, Yasovarman, charged into open battle, hoping to overwhelm Lalitaditya with sheer numbers. But Lalitaditya was well-prepared.

On the battlefield, Lalitaditya's forces pretended to retreat. Yasovarman's army chased them—right into a trap! Hidden in dense forests, archers attacked with their bows and arrows, while the cavalry—warriors on horses—cut off their escape. Victory came easily, and Yasovarman was captured.

But instead of punishing him, Lalitaditya surprised everyone. 'A great ruler fights for his people, not for personal gain,' he said. Offering Yasovarman a treaty of peace, Lalitaditya ensured that Kanauj remained autonomous but became his ally. After the campaign, Lalitaditya focused on strengthening trade and cultural ties, bringing prosperity to both regions.

Conquest of Sindh

After the victory in Kanauj, Lalitaditya turned his attention to Sindh, a land controlled by the powerful

Arab Umayyad. Sindh was rich and strategically located—a prize worth claiming. Knowing the Arab forces were disciplined and skilled, Lalitaditya devised a clever strategy.

At his war council, he addressed his commanders. 'The Arab cavalry is unstoppable on open plains,' he began, gesturing to a map. 'But here, near the Indus, the terrain will be our ally. We will lure them into the marshes where their strength becomes their weakness.'

One commander hesitated. 'Maharaja, if our men retreat, won't they lose heart?'

Lalitaditya's voice was calm but firm. 'They trust us because we plan wisely. Victory will restore their spirit.'

And so, the plan unfolded. Lalitaditya's troops pretended to flee, drawing the Arab horsemen into the marshy banks of the Indus. Suddenly, the ground beneath them changed! The powerful horses struggled as their hooves sunk deep into the soft, marshy ground. For Lalitaditya's army, it was just the moment to strike! Arrows rained down, as the young prince led the final charge. The enemy was defeated.

After the victory, his advisor Chandra spoke up. 'Maharaja, your strategy was bold, but the risk was great.'

'Great risks lead to great unity,' Lalitaditya replied. 'Divided, we fall. Together, we rise.'

Vision in Stone and Spirit

Lalitaditya's conquests were not his only achievement. He dreamt of a kingdom where culture, knowledge, and unity thrived alongside military might. Under his reign, Kashmir entered a golden era of art, architecture, and learning.

His most iconic creation was the Martand Sun Temple, an architectural marvel perched atop a hill

Exploring India's Sun Temples

Many ancient civilizations had temples to honour the sun. But did you know India has several magnificent sun temples too?

Your mission:

- Research the sun temples of Modhera, Konark, and the temples of Kumbakonam.
- What makes each of them unique?
- Do they have anything in common with sun temples from other ancient cultures, like those in Egypt, Greece, or the Americas?

with breath-taking views of the valley. The temple was dedicated to the Sun god, Surya. Its blend of Gandharan, Gupta, and Central Asian styles reflected the diversity of cultures Lalitaditya had come across during his campaigns.

Once, during a visit to the construction site, Lalitaditya said to his chief architect. 'This temple must be more than stone and mortar,' he said, his gaze fixed on the rising spires—tall, pointed structures reaching towards the sky. 'It must inspire our people to reach for the heavens, to believe in the strength of unity and beauty.' When completed, the temple was more than just a place for worship. It became a symbol of cultural pride, attracting scholars, artists, and travellers from faraway lands.

But Lalitaditya's vision stretched far beyond temples. He built cities, canals, and fortifications too. He welcomed scholars and artists in his court, turning Kashmir into a place buzzing with ideas and creativity. Under his patronage, literature, and music thrived. Poets composed verses about his victories, artisans created intricate sculptures, and philosophers debated ideas from distant lands.

Trade brought exotic goods and new ideas to Kashmir.

Through his contributions, Lalitaditya built more than a kingdom—he left behind a legacy that transcended his lifetime, proving that true greatness lies in uplifting the soul of a nation.

Amazing Architecture

Lalitaditya built incredible structures across his kingdom. One of his most fascinating creations was a special statue of Naṛhari (a form of Vishnu) in Strirajya. It was designed to float in mid-air, held up by powerful magnets placed above and below! This shows just how advanced art and technology were during his time.

Lalitaditya's Rise from Loss

Remember that even the strongest leaders face heartbreak. Lalitaditya's triumphs were shadowed by the loss of his closest friend and trusted general, Keshava. More than a commander, Keshava was a friend, a brother, a constant companion to him. So, when Keshava fell in battle, it struck Lalitaditya to his core.

For days, the king withdrew, lost in grief. Even his advisors hesitated to disturb him. It was his queen who finally approached him, finding him sitting alone, staring at Keshava's sword.

'Why does destiny take the best among us?' Lalitaditya murmured, his voice laced with grief.

The queen knelt beside him. 'Keshava gave his life for what you both believed in—a united land. Would he want you to stop now?'

Her words struck a chord. Rising from sorrow, Lalitaditya channelled his grief into action. He poured his energy into reforming his administration. He reformed the way his kingdom was run, strengthening governance and improving communication between provinces. With these changes, his land became stronger and more united than ever.

When asked how the reforms would honour Keshava's memory, Lalitaditya replied, 'By ensuring our dream outlives us both. Strength lies in building a system, not in any one person.'

Lalitaditya's *Digvijaya*: A Journey of Conquest

Lalitaditya's dream of a united and prosperous Bharat extended beyond Kashmir. Determined to bring far-flung regions together with a shared dream, he embarked on a grand *digvijaya*—a campaign of conquest and unification. His journey took him through the fertile plains of northern India, the central plateaus, and even to the borders of Central Asia.

Before setting out, he gathered his commanders. 'This is a mission to weave the scattered threads of our land into a single fabric of strength and harmony. Remember, our goal is not just to win but to unite.'

In the Deccan, local rulers resisted his advance. But rather than resorting to war that would cost countless lives, Lalitaditya opted for diplomacy. He invited their king for negotiations under a banner of peace.

'Why shed blood when unity can bring prosperity to us all?' he asked, offering an alliance that respected the autonomy of the Deccan rulers while strengthening its ties to his kingdom. Impressed by his wisdom, the king joined forces with Lalitaditya.

In the northwest, the campaign took a more warlike turn. Facing fierce resistance from tribal confederacies,

Lalitaditya's forces employed strategic brilliance to overcome their opponents. At one point, his general expressed doubt about continuing through the harsh mountain terrain.

'Maharaja, the mountains test even the strongest armies,' he cautioned.

Lalitaditya replied with unwavering determination, 'The mountains test not just armies but the resolve of a leader. If we falter now, we fail our mission.' And, so, they pressed on, securing victory.

Pushing into Central Asia, Lalitaditya brought together diverse cultures and strengthened trade ties. His ability to adapt—combining diplomacy with military strength—ensured his success. Indeed, through his *digvijaya*, Lalitaditya proved that true leadership proved the power of vision, resilience, and unity.

Learn More About Lalitaditya Muktapida

Written Records

- Lalitaditya's story comes from ancient texts, especially *Rajatarangini*, written by Kalhana in the 12th century.
- Kalhana described him as a great king who expanded his empire and enriched Kashmir's culture.

- The chronicle mixes history with legend, so scholars today compare it with other evidence.
- Kalhana emphasized that history speaks through stories, inscriptions, and ruins, inspiring future generations.

Excavations and Archaeological Evidence

- The Martand Sun Temple's ruins reveal a blend of Gandharan and Gupta influences, showing cultural exchanges.
- Inscriptions and carvings at temple sites offer insights into Lalitaditya's vision and his era.
- Historians analyse trade records, ancient coins, and foreign texts to verify details of his reign.

Miraculous Abilities

Kalhana's *Rajatarangini* tells us that Lalitaditya had incredible powers. One chilly day, while camped near the eastern ocean, he suddenly wished for *kapittha* fruits—even though they weren't in season and didn't grow there. Amazingly, a messenger from the gods appeared with the fruits! He explained that because of Lalitaditya's past kindness, he had been granted a hundred heavenly wishes. But the messenger also warned him not to waste them on small desires.

Everyday Heroes and Leadership

Lalitaditya valued everyone who kept his kingdom running. Who helps you every day?

Your Everyday Heroes

List five people who make your school day possible—bus drivers, staff, or family. How can you show them appreciation? A thank you, a note, or even a smile perhaps?

King or Queen for a Day

If you ruled like Lalitaditya, what would you do to help others? What rules would you create—or avoid? Write down your ideas.

Design Your Own Fort

Materials needed: Paper, colouring supplies, craft materials (optional)

Lalitaditya built the magnificent Martand Sun Temple. Imagine you're a royal architect. Design your own fort or temple on paper.

- What special features would make it strong?
- How would you decorate it?
- Where would you build it— on a mountain, near a river, etc.?

Present your design to your parents and explain why each feature is important.

Royal Message Delivery

Materials needed: Paper, pen, small containers

In ancient times, kings like Lalitaditya sent important messages across their kingdoms. Create a secret message system with your parents.

- Write short messages or instructions on small pieces of paper.
- Hide them around your home or garden.
- Create a simple map showing where each message is hidden.
- Take turns following the map and collecting the messages.

Once all messages are found, arrange them to reveal a complete story or instruction.

Further Reading

- *Kalhana's Rajatarangini: A Chronicle of the Kings of Kashmir* (Translated by M.A. Stein), (Oxford University Press, 1900).

- *The History and Culture of the Indian People: The Age of Imperial Kanauj,* Edited by R.C. Majumdar (Bharatiya Vidya Bhavan, 1955).
- *India: A History,* by John Keay (Grove Press, 2001).
- *The Sun Temple at Martand: Reflections on Art and Architecture,* by M.K. Dhavalikar (Indian Council of Historical Research, 1986).
- *Ancient India,* by R.S. Sharma (National Council of Educational Research and Training (NCERT), 2005).
- Vikram Sampath, *Bravehearts of Bharat: Vignettes from Indian History*, Penguin India, 2022.

Coins of the Karkota dynasty

2000 CE
1800 CE
1600 CE
1471 - 1529 CE
1400 CE
1200 CE
1000CE
800 CE

Krishnadevaraya

The Warrior King Who Rocked Vijayanagara (1471–1529 CE)

Have you ever looked closely at a fifty-rupee note? If you have, you might have noticed a special carving—the magnificent stone chariot of Hampi. This exquisite structure, part of the grand Vittala Temple complex, looks as if its stone wheels could roll away at any moment. It is a reminder of the incredible Vijayanagara empire, a kingdom known for its stunning temples, bustling markets, and mighty rulers.

Long ago, Hampi (in present-day Karnataka) was a city of wonders. Visitors from faraway lands were amazed by its golden palaces, jewel-filled markets, and grand festivals where elephants, dressed in gold, marched through the streets. The Persian ambassador, Abdur Razzaq, wrote about its riches, and a Portuguese traveller, Domingo Paes, described its towering temples and vibrant celebrations.

At the heart of this magnificent city stood the royal palace—a sprawling complex of courtyards, halls, and pavilions, surrounded by lush gardens and fountains. Emperor Krishnadevaraya sat with his clever court jester, Tenali Rama. They rested on a cool stone bench, watching the sun set over a serene lotus pond. A sweet scent of jasmine wafted through the air.

Krishnadevaraya turned to Tenali with a thoughtful look. 'Have you ever wondered what makes a leader truly great?'

Tenali, always quick with his wit, scratched his chin. 'Greatness, Rayadu?' he said, using the Telegu word for king in his address. 'Perhaps it is the size of their country?'

'No, my friend. It is something far greater. Let me tell you a story....'

Lessons from the Past

It was a warm afternoon in the grand court of Emperor Krishnadevaraya. The majestic hall was alive with activity—ministers debated important matters, scribes hurried to record royal decrees, and the air buzzed with the energy of a thriving empire.

In the midst of it all, Tenali Rama, the king's sharp-witted jester and advisor, sat cross-legged on the marble floor, his eyes twinkling with curiosity.

Krishnadevaraya leaned back thoughtfully. 'Ah, Tenali, today, my mind is travelling back in time. I have been thinking about how this great empire was built—and the lessons I have learned from life's toughest moments.'

Tenali grinned. 'Perfect timing, Rayadu! Your stories are the best, especially for the younger generation. Why not share them with me? I will pass them along, woven with a bit of my wit, of course!'

The emperor chuckled. 'Very well, Tenali. Let us begin at the beginning!'

Hampi's landscape with the Virupaksha temple

Humble Beginnings

Tenali Rama tilted his head. 'Rayadu, you sit on the throne of one of the greatest empires in history. Riches, armies, power—everything at your command! But surely life wasn't always this grand?'

Krishnadevaraya leaned back, a knowing smile on his face. 'Indeed, Tenali! My beginnings were far from grand. My early days were nothing like what you see today.'

'Ah, then tell me, Your Majesty—was there a grand adventure in a glittering palace?'

Krishnadevaraya chuckled. 'An adventure? Yes. A palace? No. My father, Narasa Nayaka, was a general—always on the battlefield. I was born into uncertainty, where the clash of swords was as common as temple bells. My childhood was spent watching my father defend our lands from constant attacks.'

'A prince born on a battlefield!' Tenali exclaimed. 'That sounds like the beginning of a hero's tale!'

The king shook his head. 'It was more about endurance than heroics, Tenali. I saw soldiers march off to war—some returning victorious, others never returning at all. From a young age, I understood the weight of war and leadership.'

'Did you always dream of being king, Rayadu?' Tenali asked.

The emperor laughed. 'No, Tenali. My only dream was to protect my family and our people. My father used to say, "A leader isn't born with a throne beneath him. He must earn the right to sit on it." That lesson stayed with me.'

'And life tested you, didn't it? I've heard stories of the struggles your family faced.'

Krishnadevaraya's face turned serious. 'After my father passed, my older brother, Vira Narasimha, took the throne. But it was a time of chaos. Our enemies—the Bahmani Sultanate and the Gajapatis of Odisha—saw us as weak and attacked. I was young, but I watched and learned. I realized that strength isn't just about fighting—it is about standing firm even when everything seems to be falling apart.'

Tenali's brow furrowed. 'But where did you find the courage, Rayadu?'

The king's voice softened. 'Courage often comes from those around us. My mother, Nagala Devi, was my pillar of strength. She told me stories of great rulers, especially King Rama, who never wavered in his duty, no matter how hard things got.'

'What did she tell you?'

'She would say that if you carry your duty like a shield, no weapon can harm you. Her words were like a flame, guiding me in my journey. I still remember the day I rallied a group of frightened soldiers. I was barely a teenager then. I climbed onto a rock and shouted, "Do not fear! This land is our mother, and we are her children. If we don't defend her, who will?" That was the first time I understood the power of words.'

Tenali grinned. 'A glimpse of the great king you would become! But tell me, Rayadu, did those early struggles ever make you bitter?'

The king shook his head. 'No, Tenali. They made me determined. Hardships are like a blacksmith's kiln—they shape your strength and character. Those years taught me the value of perseverance, loyalty, and, above all, hope.'

Tenali leaned back, smiling. 'And hope, Rayadu, is a king's greatest treasure. I see now why your people love you as much as they do.'

'Hope,' Krishnadevaraya said, 'and the will to carry out one's duty—those are the true foundations of an empire.'

A Tribute to His Mother

Krishnadevaraya built the city of Hospet (once called Nagar Hampi) to honour his mother, Nagala Devi. It became the gateway to Vijayanagara and is still an important town near the empire's ruins today.

Road to the Throne

'After my father's death, I knew the road ahead would be fraught with challenges. So, I prepared—learning about warfare, administration, diplomacy, and even languages. Those years of struggle prepared me for the greatest challenge yet.'

Tenali leaned in. 'That must have helped, my king. But no lesson can prepare you for the weight of an entire empire.'

Krishnadevaraya nodded. 'You are right, Tenali. When my brother passed away, Vijayanagara was like a boat caught in a storm. Enemies circled, and rival groups fought for power, especially the Bahmani Sultanate to the north. I had to act. I told my advisors: "A broken empire is like a shattered pot. We either leave it in pieces or rebuild it stronger." And so, we did just that.'

'What a burden to carry, Rayadu! Did it ever feel too heavy?'

Krishnadevaraya smiled. 'At times, yes. But a king must act fast. The Bahmani Sultanate thought we were weak. They were wrong!'

Tenali's eyes twinkled. 'Oh, I love a good trick, Rayadu! How did you outsmart them?'

'At the Battle of Adoni, we feigned a retreat, luring the Bahmani forces into a narrow valley. They thought they had trapped us, but we had planned it all.'

'And then?' Tenali whispered.

Krishnadevaraya's voice grew animated. 'We had hidden archers positioned on the cliffs above. Just as the Bahmani forces entered the valley, our archers unleashed a storm of arrows. Meanwhile, our cavalry swooped in, cutting off their escape and securing a decisive victory.'

Tenali clapped his hands in delight. 'A masterstroke! But, my king, battles are only part of the ruling. How did you manage the people?'

Krishnadevaraya's expression softened. 'A kingdom, Tenali, is its people. Without their trust, no army or fort can hold an empire together. I often disguised myself and walked among my subjects, listening to their concerns. On one such occasion, I met a farmer who told me his crops were failing because his village had no water. The next day, I ordered the construction of irrigation canals to ensure no farmer would ever face such hardship again.'

Tenali's admiration was clear as he said, 'You were not just a king of swords, but a king of service.'

Krishnadevaraya chuckled. 'A kingdom is strongest when it is built on the foundations of both courage and compassion, Tenali. And that is what I strive for every day.'

The Royal Agriculturist

Unlike most kings, Krishnadevaraya was deeply involved in agricultural reforms. He inspected irrigation systems himself and even joined farmers in the fields to understand their struggles.

Kondaveedu: The 'Unbreakable' Fort

'Rayadu, tell me, what about Kondaveedu? That's one of my favourite stories.'

The king leaned back, his eyes shining with the memory. 'Ah, Kondaveedu. That fort was no ordinary place. The Gajapatis thought it to be unbreakable—perched high on a hill, surrounded by cliffs. Many said it was impossible to capture.'

'Impossible?' Tenali said, raising an eyebrow. 'Surely not to you, Rayadu.'

Krishnadevaraya chuckled. 'Indeed, Tenali. To me, Kondaveedu was not a fortress. It was a test—of determination, courage, and ingenuity. Impossible is a word for those who give up too easily.'

'So what did you do?'

The king's voice grew serious. 'I studied everything—how the guards moved, the paths they took. The cliffs looked like walls, but I saw a way up. It was dangerous but not impossible!'

'And then?' Tenali leaned in.

Krishnadevaraya's voice changed, as though he was reliving the moment. 'I chose a small team of my bravest and most skilled soldiers. Under the cover of night, they began the climb with ropes and hooks. One wrong step, and they would be caught. But they made it! They reached the top, took down the guard, and opened the gates for the rest of the army. By the time the Gajapatis realized, it was over—Kondaveedu was ours!'

'Incredible! But you won more than just the fort, didn't you?'

Krishnadevaraya nodded. 'Respect, Tenali, isn't taken; it is earned. After our victory, I could have humiliated the Gajapatis. Instead, I chose peace. I married Princess Jaganmohini, the daughter of their king. That turned an enemy into a friend.'

Tenali's eyes reflected the admiration he felt for his king. 'A wise move, Your Majesty.'

The king smiled. 'A kingdom built on trust lasts longer than one built on fear. Swords and arrows can only bring temporary victories—only trust and understanding can create lasting peace.'

A King's Greatest Battle

'Rayadu,' Tenali said gently, 'not all battles are fought with swords and armies, are they?'

Mission (Im)possible! Plan Your Secret Saga

Krishnadevaraya's soldiers had to scale a cliff in the dead of night to capture Kondaveedu. Imagine you are part of the team. Can you plan your own secret mission?

Hints

- Observation First: Look around your home or school. If you had to sneak past without being noticed, what path would you take?
- Silent Steps: Try walking across a room without making a sound. Can you do it? What helps?
- Draw Your Plan: Sketch a secret path up a high fortress (or a tree, a hill, or a castle). How would you get past the guards?
- Bonus Challenge: Write a short story about your mission to capture an 'impossible' fortress!

Krishnadevaraya looked up, a shadow of sorrow passing across his face. 'No, Tenali,' he said with a heavy sigh. 'Some battles are fought within the heart. I learned this the day I lost my son, Tirumala.'

Tenali's expression softened. 'Tirumala...,' his voice trailed off. 'The light of your life, wasn't he?'

Krishnadevaraya nodded, his gaze distant. 'He was. He brought joy to my days, and a sense of purpose to my life beyond the throne. When he passed away, it felt as though the very foundation of my world had crumbled. For days, I could not bring myself to step into the court or face my people. It seemed as if the purpose of my existence had been snuffed out like a candle in the wind.'

Tenali, known for his sharp wit, now spoke with uncharacteristic gentleness. 'That must have been a burden too heavy for even the mightiest emperor to bear.'

'It was,' Krishnadevaraya admitted, his voice tinged with pain. 'But the hardest battle was yet to come—I turned against my friends and mentors, blinded by suspicion and sorrow. That, more than any war I ever fought, was my greatest defeat.'

'What did you do, Rayadu?'

'I decided to honour Tirumala's memory in a way that would serve generations to come,' the emperor said, his voice growing steadier. 'I commissioned the construction of grand temples and vast irrigation canals in his name. These projects became my solace, my way of transforming sorrow into strength. Instead of mourning him, I ensured his legacy would live on—not through tears, but through service to my people.'

'Rayadu, you turned your loss into hope for others. Just as you turn every challenge on the battlefield into a victory, you turned this grief into a triumph of the heart.'

Krishnadevaraya managed a faint smile. 'That, Tenali, is what leadership is about—finding purpose even in the darkest moments. For if a king cannot rise above his own sorrow, how can he inspire his people to do the same?'

Wisdom, Laughter, and a Lasting Legacy

The cool evening breeze rustled through the corridors of the Vijayanagara court.

'Rayadu,' he said, 'most kings spend their time in palaces—not you. You disguised yourself and walked among your people and listened to poets and scholars. Why?'

'Because, Tenali, a king's true weapon isn't his sword—it's wisdom. A strong kingdom isn't about armies and gold. It's about culture, learning, and prosperity. That's why I surrounded myself with brilliant minds like you!'

'And yet,' Tenali teased with mock humility, 'you let us poke fun at you in court!'

The king laughed heartily. 'Of course! Because humour is just as important as wisdom. A king who can laugh at himself understands his people better.'

Tenali's eyes twinkled. 'But let's not forget the beautiful legacy you are leaving behind—your temples, palaces, and monuments. The very stones of Hampi sing your praises.'

Krishnadevaraya smiled warmly. 'Wars may be forgotten, but beauty and wisdom last forever. That is a king's true legacy, Tenali.'

Coins with Deities

Krishnadevaraya issued gold coins called Varaha, engraved with Hindu deities like Lord Venkateswara and Goddess Lakshmi. These coins showcased his devotion and symbolized the prosperity of his reign.

A King Who Loved Stories

'Speaking of inspiration,' Tenali said, leaning forward, 'let's talk about your court. It is said to be the most magnificent in all of India.'

'I am fortunate,' Krishnadevaraya replied, 'to have the best minds of my time. My court included the *Ashta Diggajas*, the eight legendary poets of Telugu literature. Among them was Allasani Peddana, who wrote *Manucharitramu*, a masterpiece that still inspires readers today. I, too, contributed to literature with *Amuktamalyada*, a story of devotion and duty.'

'*Amuktamalyada* is about the sacrifices of a king, isn't it?' Tenali said.

'Yes,' the king nodded. 'A king's life is not his own—it belongs to his people. I wanted to share this truth through literature.'

'And you encouraged poets in other languages too, right?' Tenali asked.

'Of course! Our empire is home to many cultures, so I support writers in Telugu, Kannada, Sanskrit, and Tamil. Stories bring people together, Tenali. That is why they matter so much!'

Magic of Hampi

Tenali's eyes gleamed with excitement. 'Rayadu, Hampi is the city of dreams! Its temples and markets are like poetry carved in stone. The stone chariot looks so real—one might think it could roll away at any moment.'

'That was the genius of our architects,' Krishnadevaraya said proudly. 'They combined imagination with precision. The Hazara Rama temple, for example, tells the stories of the Ramayana through its carvings. Every stone has a story to tell.'

'But Hampi wasn't just about temples,' Tenali added. 'It is one of the richest cities in the world.'

Krishnadevaraya nodded. 'Trade makes it so. Merchants from Persia, China, and Portugal fill our markets with silk, spices, and jewels. I make sure that our city's wealth is reflected in its grand bazaars, gardens, and even our water canals.'

'And let's not forget the Mahanavami Dibba, your festival platform,' Tenali teased.

'Ah yes! That is where we celebrate our festivals. Festivals bring people together, Tenali. A united empire is a strong empire.'

Journey Through Hampi: Create Your Travel Journal

Imagine visiting Hampi, the grand capital of Krishnadevaraya's empire.

- If you can visit, keep a journal of what you see and feel. Draw sketches of temples, markets, or statues that fascinate you.
- If you can't visit, research Hampi online or in books. Create a mini travel journal with drawings and notes on what you've learned.
- Turn your journal into a booklet and share it with your class.

Power of Creativity

Tenali's voice turned serious. 'Rayadu, if you could teach young minds one lesson about art and architecture, what would it be?'

'That creativity is just as important as courage. A poem, a painting, or a temple—they all uplift the soul. A leader must nurture culture, for it binds people together and reminds them of their shared heritage.'

'And perhaps build a stone chariot or two?' Tenali quipped.

Krishnadevaraya laughed. 'Why not? If it inspires future generations, then it's worth it. After all, true greatness lies not just in conquest but in creation.'

Lessons for Young Readers

Tenali tilted his head thoughtfully. 'Rayadu, if you could share lessons with children today, what would they be?'

Krishnadevaraya leaned forward. 'Courage, Tenali. Life will always have challenges, big or small. True bravery is not about never feeling scared—it is about facing it anyway.'

'And creativity too, right?' Tenali asked, raising an eyebrow.

'Absolutely,' Krishnadevaraya said. 'Think outside the box. At Kondaveedu, we won not with brute force but with clever strategy. Creativity and intelligence often triumph over strength.'

'And kindness?' Tenali prompted.

The king smiled. 'A leader must serve with compassion. I learned this from walking among my people in disguise. I saw their struggles and realized that a kingdom is only as strong as the happiness of its people.'

'Don't forget humour, Rayadu!' Tenali added with a grin.

'Of course, Tenali. Laughter makes life's burdens lighter. So I would say to every child: cultivate courage, creativity, compassion, curiosity—and yes, a touch of humour. These are the qualities of a great leader.'

Learn More About Krishnadevaraya

Historical Accounts

Portuguese traveller Domingo Paes wrote about the splendour of Krishnadevaraya's court, his military strength, and his governance.

Other foreign visitors also recorded glimpses of Vijayanagara's prosperity under his rule.

Inscriptions and Temples

Inscriptions on temples and monuments highlight his contributions to architecture, religion, and administration.

Many temples he built still stand today, showcasing his devotion and vision.

Literary Contributions, Legends, and Stories

Krishnadevaraya was a poet and scholar. His famous work *Amuktamalyada* in Telugu speaks about devotion, duty, and good governance.

He supported poets and scholars, making Vijayanagara a hub of literature and learning.

Folk tales and Tenali Rama stories keep his wit and wisdom alive. Through these stories, his leadership and values continue to inspire generations.

Krishnadevaraya's Wisdom: Reflect and Discuss

The dialogues in this chapter are inspired by *Amuktamalyada*, where Krishnadevaraya shares his thoughts on being a good king.

- Which part of his ideas did you find most meaningful? Why?
- Was there anything you didn't agree with? Explain.

Discuss with a friend!

Stone Chariot Challenge

Materials needed: Building blocks, LEGO, or clay

- The stone chariot at Hampi is so amazing that it appears on the fifty-rupee note! Build your own version of the chariot using blocks, LEGO, or clay.
- Make it as detailed as possible, and see if you can make the wheels look like they could roll.
- Once complete, tell the story of where your chariot would travel and what it would see.

Tenali Rama's Wit

Materials needed: Paper, pen

Tenali Rama was known for his clever solutions to problems. With your parents, write down 3–5 problems that need solving. For example:

- How to keep monkeys from stealing fruits from the palace garden.
- How to convince a stubborn elephant to cross a bridge.
- How to tell which advisor is not telling the truth.

Take turns being Tenali Rama and coming up with the cleverest solution to each problem. Vote on whose solution was the most creative and practical!

Further Reading

- Abhijeeth Hiliyana, *Krishna Deva Raya: The Boy Who Would Be King*, Hachette India, 2022.
- Srinivas Reddy, *Raya: Krishnadevaraya of Vijayanagara*, Juggernaut, 2020.
- Pradeep Chakravarthy, *Leadership Shastra: Lessons from Indian History*, Penguin India, 2021.

Royal emblem of the Vijayanagara dynasty

2000 CE
1800 CE
1622 - 1672 CE
1600 CE
1400 CE
1200 CE
1000CE
800 CE

Lachit Borphukan

The Fearless Hero Who Fought for Assam (1622–1672 CE)

Long ago, the mighty Ahom kingdom flourished in a land of misty mountains and green valleys. Nestled along the great Brahmaputra river, this land became home to the Ahoms, who arrived in 1228 CE from the distant Shan region (now in Myanmar). They were led by their wise and fearless leader, Sukapha.

For nearly 600 years, the Ahoms ruled Assam with strength and wisdom. Unlike many other rulers in India, the Ahoms defended their land for centuries, even resisting the invading Mughals. The Ahoms were known for their administrative systems, military strength, and ability to bring together people from different communities under one rule. The Ahom kings built a strong and prosperous kingdom that was rich in trade, culture, and tradition.

The Ahoms were not just warriors but also skilled builders and innovators. They constructed strong forts using bamboo, wood, and clay to withstand Assam's heavy rains. Their soldiers, trained and familiar with the land, were fierce in battle.

But by the mid-17th century, a great danger loomed. The Mughals, the most powerful force in India at the time, had set their eyes on Assam! It was during this time of great danger that Lachit Borphukan rose to

Lead Like Lachit

Step into the boots of the great Lachit Borphukan! Can you inspire your troops, strategize for battle, and defend your land?

Battle Speech Challenge: Write and deliver a powerful speech as Lachit before the Battle of Saraighat! Stand in front of a mirror, record yourself, and analyse your performance. Learn to speak with confidence!

defend his people. Lachit was not just a commander—he was a leader who loved his land, valued his people, and believed in serving his kingdom with all his heart. His courage and wisdom would go on to save the Ahom kingdom from certain defeats and ensure its independence for years to come.

This is the story of Lachit Borphukan, the brave defender of Assam.

Making of a Hero

In the beautiful green valleys of Assam, where the mighty Brahmaputra flowed like a silver ribbon, a boy named Lachit was born in 1622. The land was rich with forests, mountains, and rivers, and its people were proud, hardworking, and fiercely independent. Lachit's father, Momai Tamuli Borbarua, was a respected minister and the commander-in-chief of the Ahom kingdom, serving under King Pratap Singha.

From a young age, Lachit saw his father working tirelessly for the kingdom. Soldiers came and went, battle reports filled the air, and the clinking of swords was a familiar sound. But one lesson stood out above all others—loyalty to the land and its people.

The Ahom palace and the Brahmaputra river

'Lachit,' his father often said, 'a leader must be brave like a lion, wise like a teacher, and humble like a servant.'

One day, when Lachit was about ten years old, he saw his father leading a meeting of soldiers. Fascinated by their shining armour and serious faces, he asked, 'Father, why do soldiers train so hard? Isn't peace better than war?'

Momai Tamuli knelt beside his son. 'Peace is precious, my child. But to protect peace, we must always be prepared. When enemies try to take what is ours, we must stand together to defend it.'

Lachit grew up with these words etched in his heart. Under his father's watchful eye, he studied not just warfare but also administration, law, and history. He trained with swords, learned to ride horses, and became a skilled archer. He would spend hours practising under the hot sun, knowing that one day, he might be called to serve his land.

As he grew older, Lachit's intelligence, discipline, and sense of justice became well known. When he came of age, he was given a position of great trust—the king's royal bodyguard, known as *soladhara barua*. It was here that Lachit proved his worth.

Rise of a Leader

Lachit Borphukan's journey as a leader began during one of Assam's most critical times in history. By the mid-17th century, the Ahom kingdom faced a formidable threat from the Mughal emperor Aurangzeb. Assam, with its fertile lands and control over the Brahmaputra, became an obvious target.

The Mughals had already captured Guwahati, which was not just a strategic location but the gateway to the rest of the Ahom kingdom. Losing this key city left the Ahoms vulnerable and shaken. King Chakradhwaj Singha, who ruled Assam at the time, knew he needed someone exceptional to lead the fight to reclaim Guwahati. Among the nobles, ministers, and generals, one name stood out—Lachit Borphukan.

One day, Lachit was summoned to the royal court.

The king looked at him with firm resolve and said, 'Lachit, I am entrusting you with the future of our land. The Mughals have taken Guwahati, but we will not let them hold it. You are now the "Borphukan", the supreme commander of our army. Lead our people, and reclaim what is ours!'

Lachit bowed deeply, his voice steady. 'Your Majesty, I will serve Assam with my life. We will drive the Mughals from our land.'

Being 'Borphukan' was more than leading an army—it required strategy, diplomacy, and administrative skills. Lachit took his duty seriously. He spent days studying the Mughal forces and identifying their weaknesses. He then reorganized the Ahom army, training soldiers to fight with discipline and precision. He inspected weapons, secured food supplies, and boosted the morale of the troops.

Lachit also rallied local chieftains and villagers. 'This is not just a war for kings and soldiers,' he declared. 'This is a fight for our homes, our freedom, and our future!' His words ignited courage. Farmers, merchants, and villagers stepped forward, offering resources, labour, and unwavering support.

Under his leadership, the Ahom army became a disciplined and motivated force. United and prepared, it stood ready for battle—a test of Lachit's skill, resilience, and determination. The battle for Guwahati was about to begin!

The Battle for Guwahati

On the eve of the battle, the king addressed him with grave concern. 'Lachit, the Mughal forces are strong, and they believe we are weak. We must reclaim our land, for Assam's future rests on this city.'

Lachit bowed respectfully and declared, 'We may not have the numbers the Mughals do, but we know our land and rivers better. I will not rest until Guwahati is ours again.' And, so, with the king's blessing, Lachit began preparations. Gathering his generals, he outlined his plan.

'We cannot fight them head-on,' he said. 'The Mughals are powerful on open ground, but they are strangers here. We will use our knowledge of the river and forests to our advantage. We will weaken them, one step at a time.'

The generals nodded in agreement.

General Chetia asked, 'What do you propose, Borphukan?'

'We will pursue their supply lines and cut off their reinforcements. Small groups of soldiers will launch surprise attacks at night. Their cannons are strong, but they cannot fire in the dark.'

The Ahom soldiers began their operations. Moving silently through dense forests and hidden river paths, they attacked Mughal supply caravans, destroyed outposts, and disrupted communications. The Mughals, though strong, grew restless and frustrated.

One night, as Lachit inspected his troops near the river, a soldier approached him.

'Borphukan, the enemy has sent reinforcements. They are gathering near the northern bank.'

Lachit's face remained calm. 'Good. Let them come. We will be ready.'

At dawn, Lachit struck. His soldiers, hidden in the narrow bends of the Brahmaputra, launched a surprise attack. Small Ahom boats cut off Mughal reinforcements before they could reach the main army. Unfamiliar with the treacherous currents of the river, the Mughals panicked.

As weeks passed, their supplies ran low and their soldiers grew tired and demoralized. Sensing the right moment, Lachit gathered his generals. 'The time has come. We will strike with full force! The enemy's defences are crumbling. Let us reclaim what is ours!'

Led by Lachit, the Ahoms launched their attack on Guwahati. The Mughals, caught off guard, tried to hold their ground, but the Ahoms fought with unmatched determination. Small, agile Ahom boats struck Mughal warships, setting them aflame with burning arrows. On land, Lachit's forces breached the Mughal fortifications with precision.

Amid the battle, Lachit's voice rose above the chaos.

'For Assam! For our freedom! Fight with all your strength!'

Inspired by their leader, the Ahom soldiers pressed forward. The overwhelmed Mughals began to retreat. When the dust settled, the Ahoms stood victorious.

'Borphukan, Guwahati is ours again. You have saved Assam!'

Lachit turned to his men. 'The victory belongs to all of you. Remember, we did not fight for glory but for our people and our land. Let this be a lesson to any who dare threaten Assam again.'

The news of the victory spread across the kingdom like wildfire. Bells rang in temples, and people celebrated Lachit Borphukan as a hero. King Chakradhwaj Singha praised Lachit's leadership, calling him the protector of Assam. But Lachit remained humble.

The battle for Guwahati was more than a military victory—it was a symbol of the Ahom spirit. For Lachit, it was only the beginning of his fight to defend Assam's freedom, a fight that would soon lead to his greatest challenge—the Battle of Saraighat.

A Smart Fort Builder

Lachit Borphukan wasn't just a great warrior—he was also a brilliant planner. Before the Battle of Saraighat, he built many forts along the Brahmaputra River to protect Assam from the Mughals. He used local materials like bamboo, clay, and wood, making the forts strong and well-hidden in the natural landscape. His clever designs helped his army defend their land.

Battle Strategy Challenge

Imagine you are the commander of an army preparing for battle. You don't just need warriors—you need strategy!

- Draw a Battle Plan: Sketch a simple map of a fort or battlefield. Where would you place your soldiers? Where would you hide supplies?
- Train Like a Warrior: Try doing 10 jumping jacks, 5 squats, and 3 minutes of running in place. How does it feel? A real warrior trains every day!
- Rally Your People: Imagine you have to give a speech to inspire your town. What would you say? Write or say it out loud!

The Battle of Saraighat

In 1671, the Mughal emperor Aurangzeb sent his most trusted general, Ramsingh I, to capture Assam again. This time, too, the Mughal army was enormous. Their target was clear—the Brahmaputra river, the lifeline of the Ahom kingdom.

Lachit Borphukan gathered his generals. 'The Mughals are mighty on land, but we will fight them on water. The Brahmaputra will be our battlefield, and the river will fight alongside us.'

The Mughals attacked with massive warships, sure of their victory! But the Ahoms were ready. Lachit had ordered the construction of small, agile boats that could outwit the Mughals. Hidden in the river's bends, Ahom archers waited, bows drawn.

As the Mughal fleet approached, Lachit stood on his boat. 'Brothers! Let us show the Mughals the strength of Assam!' And, so, the Ahoms struck. Their boats weaved through the enemy fleet, archers firing flaming arrows. Mughal ships burst into flames. Soldiers jumped into the water, swords and spears clashing.

Then disaster struck! Lachit burned with fever.

His generals pleaded with him. 'Borphukan, you are not well. Let us fight this battle in your name.'

His eyes blazed. 'How can I rest when my land is under attack? I will fight, even if it costs me my life!'

Carried onto a boat, Lachit led the final charge. Inspired, his men fought harder. The Mughals, unable to navigate their large ships, crumbled. By evening, the Brahmaputra flowed once again under the Ahom flag.

Lachit's leadership and clever strategy saved Assam. The victory at Saraighat became legend—proof that courage and intelligence could defeat even the mightiest enemy.

A Hero's Final Stand

But Lachit's victory came at a heavy price. His fever worsened, and his body grew weaker by the day. One evening, as he rested by the Brahmaputra, his loyal soldier Tularam sat beside him.

'Borphukan, your bravery has saved Assam. The people are singing songs of your heroism.'

Lachit smiled faintly. 'It was not just me, Tularam. It was the courage of our people, the unity of our soldiers, and the blessings of our land.'

Tularam's eyes brimmed with tears. 'You gave everything for Assam.'

Lachit placed a weary hand on his shoulder. 'A leader's duty is to serve, no matter the sacrifice. If Assam is safe, my work is done.'

A few days later, in 1672, Lachit Borphukan passed. As the sun set over the Brahmaputra, the people of Assam gathered to honour their hero. Songs of his bravery echoed across the land, his name forever etched in the hearts of the people he fought to protect.

A Leader Who Put Duty First

Before the Battle of Saraighat, Lachit discovered that his own uncle had been careless while building a fort, causing delays. Without hesitation, he ordered his execution, saying, 'My uncle is not more important than my motherland!' This showed his unwavering commitment to duty and his belief that everyone, no matter their relation, must be accountable in times of war.

Lachit's Legacy Lives on

Today, Lachit Borphukan's name stands as a symbol of courage and sacrifice. The victory at Saraighat remains one of India's most remarkable military triumphs. To honour him, the Lachit Borphukan Maidam was built in Jorhat, where his remains rest. Every year on 24 November, Assam celebrates Lachit Divas as a tribute to his contributions.

His legacy reaches beyond Assam. The Lachit Borphukan Gold Medal, awarded to the best cadet at the National Defence Academy (NDA), reminds future leaders of his bravery and dedication.

His story proves that true leadership is not about power but inspiring and uniting others. With determination and love for one's land, even the strongest enemies can be defeated. As long as the Brahmaputra flows and the people of Assam sing his name, Lachit Borphukan will live on—forever inspiring generations to defend what they hold dear.

Learn More About Lachit Borphukan

Historical Records

- The *Ahom Buranjis*, historical chronicles written in the now-extinct Ahom language and Assamese, document Lachit's leadership and the Battle of Saraighat.
- Even Mughal historians recorded his brilliance, acknowledging his tactics in Persian accounts of Ramsingh I's campaign.

Memorials and Monuments

- The Lachit Borphukan Maidam in Jorhat marks his final resting place and stands as a reminder of his sacrifice and service to the land.
- Every year, people gather at this site to pay their respects.

Oral Traditions

- In Assamese villages, folk songs and stories about Lachit continue to be passed down through generations.
- Elders recount how, even in sickness, he stood firm on the battlefield to protect his people.
- Lachit's story lives on—not just in history books, but in the hearts and voices of the people he fought for.

Warriors from Your Land

What is your mother tongue?

In your language or the state you live in, explore the stories of brave warriors.

- What can you learn from their lives?
- How will you use that learning in your life?
- Why do wars happen—are they useful or not? Discuss this with your parents.

River Strategy Game

Materials needed: Blue fabric/paper (for river), small toys/objects (for boats), obstacles

Lachit Borphukan used the Brahmaputra river to defeat the Mughals.

Create your own river battle strategy game:

- Lay out blue fabric or paper as your 'river'.
- Use small toys or objects as boats.
- Place 'obstacles' along the river.
- Take turns moving your boats and explaining your strategy.
- The goal is to get your boats safely across while blocking your opponent.

Discuss how geography (like rivers and mountains) helps in defence.

Leadership Speech

Materials needed: Paper, pen

Lachit was known for inspiring his soldiers with powerful speeches. Write and practice your own motivational speech for an imaginary battle. Include:

- Why you're fighting—such as to protect your home or family.

- What makes your team special.
- Why you believe you can win.

Deliver your speech to your parents with enthusiasm and confidence! Ask them to rate your speech on how inspired it made them feel afterwards.

Further Reading

- B.K. Barua, *A Comprehensive History of Assam*, Munshiram Manoharlal Publishers Pvt. Ltd, 2003.
- Suresh Sharma, *Lachit Borphukan: The Warrior of Assam*, National Book Trust, India, 2015.
- Vikram Sampath, *Bravehearts of Bharat: Vignettes from Indian History*, Penguin India, 2022.
- P.C. Kalita, *Lachit Borphukan and His Times*, Publication Board Assam, 2008.
- Pradeep Chakravarthy, *Leadership Shastra: Lessons from Indian History*, Penguin India, 2021.

Royal insignia of the Ahom dynasty

2000 CE
1800 CE
1630 -1680 CE
1600 CE
1400 CE
1200 CE
1000CE
800 CE

Chhatrapati Shivaji Maharaj

The Ultimate Strategist Who Built the Maratha Empire (1630–1680 CE)

Shivaji Bhonsle, the great Maratha leader, was one of India's most legendary rulers. In the 17th century, much of India was under the control of the Mughal Empire, but Shivaji's resistance led to the creation of the Maratha empire—also called Hindavi Swarajya—which became a symbol of defiance, bravery, and ingenuity. His story is not just about battles but inspiring people to take control of their own lives.

Shivaji's Early Years

Shivaji was born on a cool February morning in 1630 at Shivneri Fort, near Pune. His mother, Jijabai, gazed lovingly at her newborn son and whispered, 'One day, this land will look to you for hope.'

His father, Shahaji Bhonsle, a general serving the Sultanate of Bijapur, remarked. 'He will need strength and wisdom. This world is not kind to dreamers.'

When Shivaji was a young boy, Jijabai moved to Poona (now Pune) with him. There, she built Lal Mahal, a red-brick palace that became their home. Shivaji's days were filled with learning as Jijabai took great care in shaping his mind and heart.

'Listen closely, Shivaji,' she once said. 'This is the story of brave heroes who fought for justice and their land. You must grow up with their courage in your heart.' Little Shivaji listened wide-eyed, his mind alive with visions of warriors and mighty forts.

He spent his days exploring the nearby forts, racing to the top with his friends.

'One day,' he told his best friend Tanaji, 'I'll have my forts, and they'll be places of safety and strength for our people.'

'But how, Shivaji?' Tanaji asked. 'The Mughals and the sultanates are so powerful. Even your father works for them.'

Shivaji's eyes shone with determination. 'Power doesn't mean right, Tanaji. These lands belong to us, the people of Maharashtra. One day, we will build a kingdom where everyone is treated justly.'

While Shivaji dreamed of freedom, the world around him was complex. The Mughal Empire, led by Emperor Aurangzeb, was vast and strong. The Deccan sultanates, like Bijapur and Golconda, controlled southern India. Many thought Shivaji's destiny was to serve these rulers quietly, but in his heart, he knew he was meant for something greater.

Shivaji and His Mother's Teachings

Shivaji's mother, Jijabai, played a huge role in shaping him as a leader. She taught him the values of courage, justice, and love for the land. Through stories from the Ramayana and Mahabharata, she inspired him with tales of heroism and righteousness. Her wisdom and strength helped Shivaji grow into the great king he became.

Raigad Fort

Swaraj's Big Dream: Freedom for His People

As a teenager, Shivaji often sat under a large banyan tree, listening to his mother, Jijabai, tell stories of valour and justice. 'Shivaji,' she would say, 'our people deserve freedom. They should live with dignity, not under the rule of outsiders.'

These words planted a seed in Shivaji's heart. One evening, he asked his tutor, Dadoji Konddeo, 'Guruji, why must we obey rulers who do not care for our land? Why can't we govern ourselves?'

Dadoji's eyes gleamed with pride. 'That is the spirit of a true leader, Shivaji! If you believe in Swaraj, meaning self-rule, then you must fight for it.'

By fifteen, Shivaji had a plan. He gathered local boys—his friends and neighbours—and spoke with determination. 'Our land deserves freedom. We will build a force, small but fearless, and take back what is ours.'

At sixteen, he captured his first fort, Torna, hidden deep in the Sahyadri mountains. Standing atop its high walls, he declared, 'This fort shall now be called Prachandgarh, the gateway to Swaraj!'

One by one, forts fell under his control, and his dream of 'swaraj' began to come alive.

Swaraj: Your Vision of Freedom

Shivaji Maharaj's idea of Swaraj (self-rule) was about people governing themselves, free from oppression. Bal Gangadhar Tilak later invoked Shivaji's legacy to inspire India's freedom movement.

- What does freedom mean to you today?
- If you could create your own Swaraj, what rules would you set?
- How do leaders today uphold the values of self-rule and justice?

Design a poster or slogan inspired by Shivaji's vision of Swaraj. Use powerful words and symbols that represent freedom and self-rule.

The Battle of Pratapgad

The sun shone over the dense forests near Pratapgad Fort, where a tense meeting was about to take place. Shivaji adjusted his armour hidden beneath his clothes, as his trusted commanders stood nearby, their faces lined with worry.

'Raje,' said Tanaji Malusare, his loyal lieutenant, 'Afzal Khan is known for his deceit. Are you certain about this meeting?'

Shivaji smiled calmly. 'I know his plan, Tanaji. He sees me as a minor rebel, but he will learn today that underestimating your enemy can be dangerous.'

Meanwhile, Afzal Khan, the giant general of Bijapur, waited in his tent. Standing over seven feet tall, he was as strong as he was ruthless! When Shivaji entered, Khan spread his arms for an embrace, his tone smooth but insincere. 'Ah, Shivaji! Let us end this peacefully.'

As they embraced, Khan suddenly grabbed Shivaji's neck, trying to crush him. But Shivaji was ready! Swift as lightning, Shivaji struck with his *wagh nakh*—a sharp, claw-like weapon hidden in his hand. Khan staggered, wounded.

Outside, Shivaji's hidden soldiers launched a surprise attack, defeating the Bijapur army. The Battle of Pratapgad became a shining example of courage and strategy, proving that brains could defeat brute strength.

Tricking the Sultan

Meanwhile, the Bijapur Sultanate was furious with Shivaji's growing power. To stop him, the sultan captured his father, Shahaji, holding him hostage. Now Shivaji faced an impossible choice: surrender or risk his father's life!

One evening, sitting with his trusted advisors, Shivaji's brow furrowed in thought. 'If we give in, our dream of swaraj will die. But if we act recklessly, my father's life could be lost. We must tread carefully.'

'Perhaps we can trick them,' suggested one of his men. 'Pretend we are no threat to Bijapur.'

Shivaji's eyes lit up. 'Yes! We will appear small and weak while secretly building our strength.'

He then sent respectful messages to the sultan, pretending to be loyal and harmless. Meanwhile, he silently strengthened his forces and expanded his influence. After weeks of careful planning, the sultan believed Shivaji's act and released Shahaji. Shivaji's cleverness had saved his father—and his dream of swaraj remained alive!

Overcoming Struggles

But swaraj wasn't an easy target, and Shivaji had to keep working hard. One day, he gathered his men and said, 'We may not have large armies or endless wealth, but we have something more powerful—our wits and love for our land.'

Tanaji frowned. 'Shivaji Raje, how can we fight such massive armies with so few men?'

Shivaji smiled. 'We will not fight them head-on, Tanaji. That would be foolish. Instead, we'll use *ganimi kava*, or guerrilla warfare. This means we'll strike where they least expect, in the forests, on steep hills, or narrow passes. Then, we'll disappear before they can catch us.'

And so, Shivaji and his small band of warriors began their daring raids. They lured enemy forces into dangerous terrain, attacked swiftly, and vanished like the wind! Each success boosted their confidence, and even their failures became lessons.

One evening, after a difficult day, Shivaji addressed his tired men. 'Every setback makes us stronger,' he said. 'We learn, adapt, and grow. One day, the world will remember us—not for our numbers, but for our courage and strategy.'

And indeed, they did.

Guerrilla Tactics: Outsmart the Army

Shivaji mastered guerrilla warfare, using hills and forests to launch surprise attacks on larger armies. He believed, 'A small army with a sharp mind can defeat even the mightiest force.'

His strategies later inspired leaders like Rani of Jhansi and Tantia Tope during the 1857 Rebellion.

Remember Lachit Borpukhan? He too used similar tactics to defeat the Mughal army at the Battle of Saraighat.

Activity: Outsmart the Enemy!

You have 500 warriors against 10,000 enemies. Plan your attack.

- Where will you strike?
- What trick will you use?
- How will you escape?

Draw a battle plan or write a short strategy to outsmart the enemy—just like Shivaji and Lachit!

Brave Stand at Pawankhind

In 1660, Panhala Fort was under siege. Shivaji Maharaj and his men were by the powerful general Siddhi Johar of the Bijapur Sultanate.

'We must get Maharaj to safety!' declared Baji Prabhu Deshpande, Shivaji's loyal commander.

As Shivaji slipped away through the rugged hills, Baji Prabhu and his small band of Maratha warriors prepared to face the enemy. 'We will hold them back at Pawankhind,' Baji vowed, gripping his sword tightly.

Though outnumbered, the Marathas fought valiantly. Their heroic sacrifice gave Shivaji the time he needed to reach safety, a moment of unmatched bravery in Maratha history.

Sindhudurg: The Fort That Defied the Sea

On a breezy evening, Shivaji stood on the shores of the Arabian Sea, his eyes locked on a rocky island in the distance.

'This island will be our shield,' he declared to his commanders. 'We will build Sindhudurg Fort here to stop enemy ships and invaders from the sea.'

One commander hesitated. 'But, Maharaj, the rocks make it nearly impossible to build.'

Shivaji smiled. 'The tougher the challenge, the stronger our fort will be!'

And so it was. Carefully designed to fit the rocky terrain, Sindhudurg rose from the sea, blending into the rocky terrain. It had a hidden entrance, known only to Maratha warriors.

'No enemy shall breach these walls,' Shivaji said proudly. And none ever did.

Write Your Royal Decree

'A sword protects the kingdom, but fairness strengthens it,' Shivaji once said. He wasn't just a warrior—he was a fair and just ruler. He ensured:

- Equality: All subjects were treated fairly, regardless of background.
- Fair taxes: Farmers and traders were not overburdened.
- Strong leadership: He led by example, living simply like his soldiers.

Now, imagine you are a ruler. Your people face a drought.

- How will you help farmers?
- Will you change taxes?
- What laws will you create?

Write a royal decree explaining your decisions.

Turning Defeat into Opportunity

Aurangzeb's name struck fear across the land. But Shivaji? He refused to bow.

'Why should we fear Aurangzeb?' Shivaji asked, his eyes blazing with determination. 'If no one stands up to him, who will protect our people?'

Tanaji hesitated. 'Maharaj, Aurangzeb's armies are vast, and his reach is endless. Many kings have already surrendered.'

Shivaji smiled faintly. 'Fear is his greatest weapon, Tanaji. But we will not let fear rule us.'

Years later, his words were tested during the Siege of Purandar in 1665. Surrounded by Mughal forces, Shivaji knew he couldn't win the battle outright. 'We'll make peace now,' he said, 'but only to fight another day.' Through the Treaty of Purandar, Shivaji cleverly surrendered 23 forts but preserved his army. As part of the treaty, he was summoned to Aurangzeb's court in Agra. Treated like a captive, he realized escape was his only option.

Feigning illness, Shivaji sent baskets of fruits to the poor. But inside one of them, hidden beneath layers of offering, were Shivaji and his son! Under the guards' noses, they had slipped away! Shivaji's daring escape didn't just save his life—it reignited the fight against the Mughals.

'Aurangzeb may rule the empire,' Shivaji said on his return, 'but he'll never rule our spirit!'

In another incident, on a cold night in 1670, Shivaji and his men stood beneath the steep walls of Kondana Fort.

'We'll climb those walls and take the fort by surprise,' he said, his eyes shining with determination. Leading the charge was Tanaji Malusare.

Using ropes, they silently scaled the cliffs, taking the guards completely by surprise. A fierce battle followed, with Tanaji fighting bravely to secure the fort. But victory came at a heavy price—Tanaji lost his life. When Shivaji heard the news, he said, *'Gad ala, pan sinha gela'* thc fort is won, but the lion is lost.

Shivaji's Royal Seal

Shivaji's royal seal called the Rajmudra showed his values and vision. It had a special message in Sanskrit: 'This seal of Shivaji, son of Shahaji, will shine like the new moon. It will be honoured by all and will always work for the good of the people.' This seal was more than just a mark of his rule—it was a promise that he would always put his people first.

Dawn of a New Kingdom

It was in 1674 that Shivaji's Raigad Fort was alive with celebration.

Courtiers in silks, scholars with scrolls, and warriors in shining armour—everyone gathered to witness an extraordinary moment in history. Flags fluttered, flower garlands adorned the walls, and the air was thick with the scent of incense. In the midst of it all sat Shivaji. Draped in robes of gold and jewels.

'Baba,' a young boy whispered in the crowd, 'why is today special?'

The father smiled. 'Because today, Shivaji Maharaj becomes the first independent Hindu king in centuries. He is giving us hope for a kingdom of our own, free and strong.'

As the crown was placed on his head, Shivaji rose. 'This kingdom is not mine alone,' he declared. 'It belongs to the people. Together, we shall protect it with justice and courage!'

The ceremony marked the beginning of a new era. For the people of Maharashtra, Shivaji's coronation symbolized not just independence but also the promise of a brighter future.

However, a few years later, in 1680, Raigad fell silent. Shivaji had passed away at 50. The once vibrant courtyard was now filled with silence, broken only by the soft sobs of his followers.

'Baba,' the same boy, now older, said, 'what will happen to the kingdom now that Shivaji Maharaj is gone?'

The father's face was solemn. 'There will be uncertainty, but Shivaji Maharaj's legacy will guide us. His son, Sambhaji, will continue to fight for our freedom.'

And so it was. Sambhaji, though faced with great challenges, carried forward his father's mission, standing bravely against the Mughal Empire. The kingdom endured because of the strong foundation Shivaji had built.

Shivaji: The Founder of the Navy

Shivaji was one of the first Indian rulers to build a powerful navy. He knew that protecting the coast was just as important as guarding the land. His warships patrolled the Arabian Sea, keeping enemies like the Portuguese, Dutch, and British in check. He also built strong sea forts like Sindhudurg and Vijaydurg to defend his kingdom.

To honour his vision, the Indian Navy named a ship after him—INS Shivaji.

A Lasting Impact

Shivaji's greatest achievement was building the Maratha empire, a dream that began with his coronation and expanded under his successors. By the mid-18th century, the empire stretched across much of India, challenging the mighty Mughals.

Shivaji was also clever with foreign powers like the Portuguese and the English. He allowed them to trade but made sure they followed his rules. He knew how to gain wealth without giving away control. And he always kept the welfare of his people in mind.

Even today, Shivaji Maharaj's legacy continues to inspire. His forts, like Raigad and Sinhagad, are visited by thousands who admire his courage and vision. Monuments like the Chhatrapati Shivaji Maharaj Terminus in Mumbai and countless schools and institutions bear his name.

On Shivaji Jayanti, people celebrate his life with parades, cultural programmes, and re-enactments of his battles. His story of turning dreams into reality teaches young and old alike that courage, determination, and fairness can overcome any obstacle.

As the young boy and his father stood at Raigad Fort, the boy asked, 'Do you think I can ever be like Shivaji Maharaj?'

His father knelt beside him, looking into his eyes. 'Of course, you can. Shivaji Maharaj was born the son of a small chieftain, yet he built an empire. If you dream big, work hard, and never give up, you can achieve great things too.'

The boy nodded, his heart swelling with hope. Shivaji's story, he realized, was not just about battles or forts. It was about courage, justice, and the belief that even the humblest beginnings could lead to greatness.

Ashtapradhan Mandal: A Team of Eight

Shivaji created a special council called the Ashtapradhan Mandal, which means 'Council of Eight Ministers'. These were his most trusted advisors, each in charge of important tasks like money, law, defence, and administration. They helped him run the kingdom wisely and fairly. By sharing responsibilities, Shivaji made sure his government was strong and well-organized—a smart idea that helped his empire grow.

Learn More About Shivaji

Written Records

- *Sabhasad Bakhar*. Written in 1697 by Krishnaji Anant Sabhasad, it offers a first-hand account of Shivaji's life and campaigns.

- *Shivabharat*. This is a biography by Kavindra Parmanand, a poet in Shivaji's court.
- *A History of the Mahrattas*. This book was written by James Grant Duff in the 18th century. It is based on both Maratha and Mughal sources.

Forts, Legends, and Inspiration

- List all the forts that Shivaji captured/built. How many have you climbed?
- Visit one of his forts, draw the fort plan, and imagine how you would organize and plan various activities in the fort.
- A warrior of Maharashtra, Malik Ambar, influenced Shivaji's military tactics. Find out more about him.
- Which story from the Ramayana or Mahabharata must have inspired Shivaji to bravely face all challenges that came his way? How does it inspire you?

Secret Fortress Model

Materials needed: Cardboard box, craft supplies, scissors (with parent supervision)

Shivaji was a master of capturing and defending forts. Convert a cardboard box into a model of a secret fortress.

- Cut openings for doors and windows.
- Create secret passages or hidden rooms.
- Add defensive features like walls and lookout towers.
- Design traps for invaders.

When finished, explain to your parents how your fortress would be defended and why it would be hard to capture.

Guerrilla Tactics Game

Materials needed: Open space (indoors or outdoors), small objects to 'capture'

Shivaji used guerrilla warfare (quick surprise attacks) to defeat larger armies.

Play a strategic tag game.

- Place 5–10 small objects around a play area.
- One player is the 'defender' guarding the objects.

- The other player is Shivaji trying to capture the objects.
- Shivaji must move quietly and use strategy to capture objects without being tagged.
- Take turns being the defender and Shivaji.

Discuss what strategies worked best and why Shivaji's tactics were so effective.

Further Reading

- R.C. Majumdar, *The History and Culture of the Indian People* [Volume 7: 'The Mughul Empire' and Volume 8: 'The Maratha Supremacy, Bhartiya Vidya Bhavan'], 2001.
- Sir Jadunath Sarkar, *Shivaji and His Times*, 5th revised edition, New Delhi: Orient Blackswan, 2010.
- Pradeep Chakravarthy, *Leadership Shastra: Lessons from Indian History*, Penguin India, 2021.

Shivaji's Rajamudra (royal seal)

2000 CE
1800 CE
1725 -1795 CE
1600 CE
1400 CE
1200 CE
1000CE
800 CE

Ahilyabai Holkar

The Powerful Queen Who Ruled with Justice and Vision (1725–1795 CE)

In the busy city of Indore, one name shines brighter than the rest—Ahilyabai Holkar. She wasn't just a queen; she was a kind and wise leader, a protector, and a builder who cared deeply for her people. Even today, her name lives on in the city's schools, streets, and stories told from one generation to the next.

Ahilyabai Holkar ruled the kingdom of Malwa from 1767 to 1795, turning it into a place full of art, culture, and content people. She built temples, wells, and ghats all across India—many of which still stand today. But her greatness wasn't just in the things she built. It was in her fairness, her strength in tough times, and her deep love for her people.

Ahilyabai's journey wasn't easy. She was born in 1725 in a small village called Chaundi in Maharashtra. Her father, Mankoji Shinde, was a simple village chief, but he had big dreams for his daughter. At a time when most girls didn't go to school, he made sure she learned to read, write, and understand sacred texts. He taught her to be wise, brave, and kind.

The Holkar dynasty, into which she would later marry, had similarly humble beginnings. Malhar Rao Holkar, her future father-in-law, started his life as a farmer in the Deccan plateau. It was through determination and clever thinking that he rose to prominence under the Peshwas, becoming the subedar of Malwa. The Holkars soon earned a reputation for military skills, loyalty, and governance. He saw something special in Ahilyabai and knew she had the heart of a true leader. And he was right! One day, she would become one of the most beloved queens in India's history.

Early Life of Ahilyabai

In the quiet village of Chaundi, surrounded by lush green fields and rolling hills, a young girl named Ahilya grew up in a simple but loving home. Her father, a devout farmer, believed in the power of education—something rare for girls at the time.

'Ahilya,' he would say gently, 'you must learn to read and write. Knowledge is the light that will guide you through the darkest times.'

Ahilya listened closely, her bright eyes full of curiosity. She learned quickly, reading scriptures and asking questions about the brave and wise figures in her father's stories.

Years later, as she sat in the grand courtyard of Maheshwar Fort, listening to the Narmada river's gentle flow, she recalled those early days to her trusted general, Tukoji Rao Holkar.

'Your Highness,' Tukoji said, 'how did a girl from Chaundi become the beloved queen of the Holkar dynasty?'

Ahilyabai smiled. 'It feels like a lifetime ago, Tukoji. I was nine when fate brought Malhar Rao Holkar to

Ghats of Varanasi

our village. He had stopped at a temple where I was praying. He saw something in me—perhaps my focus or humility. He told my father, "This child has wisdom beyond her years."'

'And that's how you came to Indore?' Tukoji said.

'Yes,' she nodded. 'Malhar Rao later arranged my marriage to his son, Khanderao Holkar. That's how I became part of the Holkar family. Little did I know how my life would change!'

From Grief to Greatness

Tukoji spoke carefully. 'Your Highness, your journey to the throne was filled with sorrow. Losing your husband Khanderao must have been unbearable.'

Ahilyabai's face softened. 'It was the hardest moment of my life, Tukoji. Khanderao was not just my husband; he was my friend. He was brave, but his impulsiveness on the battlefield worried me.'

Tukoji leaned forward, his voice low with respect. 'He died during the siege of Kumbher, didn't he?'

She nodded. 'In 1754. When the news reached me, my world had shattered. I was only 29 years old, and suddenly, I was a widow. In my grief, I even thought of ending my life.'

Tukoji's eyes darkened. 'But Malhar Rao Holkar, your father-in-law, stopped you.'

'He did,' she said, a faint smile returning. 'He held my hand and said, "Ahilya, Indore needs you. You are destined for greater things." His words lit my path when all seemed dark. He treated me not as a widow, but as a leader.'

'And you stayed,' Tukoji said softly.

'I stayed,' she affirmed. 'But the grief never truly left me. I turned to prayer for strength. Slowly, I began assisting Malhar Rao in his work. He was growing old and saw that I had a mind for administration. He taught me how to rule wisely and with compassion.'

'And when Malhar Rao passed?'

'Indore faced a crisis,' she said. 'My son, Male Rao, was next in line, but he was young and unwell. The nobles whispered their doubts—could a woman rule? Some even plotted against me.'

Tukoji frowned. 'It was chaos. And then Male Rao—'

'He passed away in 1767, at just 22,' she said heavily. 'He had been sick for so long. Losing him was unbearable. He was my only son, my last hope for the future of our family. When he died, it felt like a part of me had died too.'

Her voice faltered before she straightened her shoulders and spoke. 'As a mother, I was shattered. But as a ruler, I could not let Indore suffer.'

Tukoji studied her in awe. 'How did you find the strength, Your Highness?'

'In the beginning, it felt impossible,' she admitted. 'I turned to the Bhagavad Gita: "Do your duty without attachment to the results." My people were also like my children. If I gave in to my grief, who would care for them?'

'That must have taken immense courage.'

'It did,' Ahilyabai said firmly. 'But it was necessary. Male Rao's death taught me that life is uncertain, but duty remains. I vowed to serve Indore, ensuring my people never suffered from neglect.'

'And in doing so, you became the pillar of the Holkar dynasty,' Tukoji said with admiration.

'Tragedy taught me resilience,' she said. 'Many doubted me. Some refused to follow my orders. But I studied the administration tirelessly and surrounded myself with wise advisors.'

She paused, her expression growing thoughtful. 'It was not easy, Tukoji. Many doubted me. Some said I was too soft because I was a woman. Others tested me by refusing to follow orders. But I refused to let their doubts affect me. I studied the administration tirelessly and surrounded myself with wise advisors.'

'And you ruled with justice,' Tukoji observed.

'Yes, justice was my guide,' she said. 'I wanted every farmer, merchant, soldier, and nobleman to feel heard. I held an open court every day so anyone could

Rule with Justice and Wisdom

Ahilyabai Holkar ruled with wisdom and fairness, listening to her people and making just decisions. Imagine you are a ruler.

- A farmer comes to you, saying his crops were ruined in a storm. How would you help?
- A merchant claims someone stole from his shop, but there are no witnesses. What would you do?
- Two friends argue over land they both claim. How would you settle the dispute fairly?

Discuss with a friend.

bring their problems to me. I made decisions based on fairness, not favouritism.'

Tukoji smiled. 'And the people loved you for it.'

'Love and trust are built over time,' she said. 'Even in the darkest moments, duty and hope are lights that guide us forward. That light made me the ruler my people needed.'

Tukoji bowed. 'Your Highness, your story is one of courage and grace. Indore could have had no greater protector.'

The Queen Who Won Hearts, Not Wars

Tukoji leaned forward, his eyes full of curiosity. 'There is a story everyone admires about you, Your Highness. When the nobles rebelled against you, how did you win them over?'

Ahilyabai smiled, remembering. 'Ah, yes! When I first became queen, many nobles doubted me. What can a woman do, they must have thought! Some even refused to pay taxes.'

'That must have been hard,' Tukoji said. 'What gave you the courage to face them?'

'It wasn't just courage, Tukoji. It was faith—faith in God, in justice, and my people. I knew that force would not work. A kingdom divided from within cannot stand strong. I had to unite everyone.'

Tukoji's eyes widened. 'How did you do it?'

'I invited the nobles to the palace,' Ahilyabai said. 'They expected punishment, but instead, I greeted them with respect. I listened to their complaints. Some felt taxes were too harsh on farmers. Others wanted a greater role in decision making'

'You just … listened?' Tukoji's said.

'Yes,' she nodded. 'And then I made fair changes. I introduced a better tax system to help farmers. I gave the nobles important responsibilities in administration. But I also reminded them, "Our enemies are outside the kingdom. If we fight among ourselves, we will fall."'

Tukoji smiled. 'Kindness with firmness. That's wise! Did they accept your leadership?'

'Most of them did,' Ahilyabai said. 'They saw I wasn't their enemy but their ally. We rebuilt trust, and Indore grew stronger.'

'And the people?'

'My people have always been my strength, Tukoji. A ruler must serve her people. When they saw I cared for them, they gave me their trust. That trust carried me forward.'

Tukoji shook his head in wonder. 'It's inspiring, Your Highness. You turned a rebellion into unity, without shedding a drop of blood!'

'Leadership is not about fear, Tukoji,' Ahilyabai said. 'It's about bringing people together. Hard times can break us or make us stronger. If we face challenges, they become opportunities to grow.'

Tukoji bowed his head. 'A lesson for all of us, Your Highness.'

The Queen Who Wove Her Own Clothes

Ahilyabai Holkar was a humble and simple ruler. Instead of wearing fancy clothes, she dressed in handwoven white saris—sometimes made from fabric she spun herself! This showed her belief in living simply, even as a powerful queen.

Lead with Fairness

Imagine you are a leader facing a problem. Your people are unhappy! What would you do?

Hints

Listen first: What are people upset about?

Speak next: Repeat what you heard – check if you listened correctly!

Think fairly: What changes can you make to help?

Stay strong: How will you remind everyone to work together?

Discuss with a friend.

Ahilyabai's voice turned gentle but firm. 'It is a lesson for anyone who chooses unity over division.'

As the sun dipped lower over the river, Tukoji knew there was more to this story. It was a timeless lesson in leadership.

A Queen's Greatest Treasure

Tukoji sat deep in thought, 'Your Highness, people often talk about the temples, roads, and wells you built. What made you focus on such work?'

Ahilyabai smiled. 'A ruler's wealth should not sit locked in a treasure room. It is meant to serve the people. When I built temples, I wasn't just creating places for worship—I was giving people spaces for peace, hope, and community.'

'The Kashi Vishwanath Temple in Varanasi is one of your most famous works,' Tukojji said. 'People say it was a monumental task.'

Ahilyabai's face turned serious. 'That temple had been destroyed many times by invaders. The people of Kashi had lost something sacred. Restoring it was about more than stone and walls—it was about bringing back faith.'

'But you didn't stop at temples. You built ghats and wells too.'

'Ah, yes, Tukoji! Without water, how will people survive? I built the Ganga Ghat in Varanasi, the Ahilya Ghat in Haridwar, and many wells and tanks across the kingdom. No one should go thirsty. I built dharmashalas—shelters where travellers could rest, no matter who they were or where they came from.'

Tukoji raised an eyebrow. 'Your efforts reached far beyond Indore. How did you do so much?'

'Because Tukoji, I saw all of Bharat as my family,' Ahilyabai said simply. 'That's why I helped rebuild the Somanath temple in Gujarat, the Vishnu temple in Gaya, and the Ujjain Mahakaleshwar temple. Even if the people were far away, their needs mattered to me.'

Tukoji looked around at the grand fort. 'And what about this place, Maheshwar Fort? It's a marvel of architecture.'

Ahilyabai chuckled softly. 'Maheshwar is special to me. Indore had grown too noisy and crowded. I needed a place where I could think clearly. The Narmada river gives me peace. This fort is not just my home—it is the heart of our kingdom's administration and culture.'

Tukoji was impressed. 'You balanced devotion and governance so effortlessly, Your Highness.'

'That's because devotion is governance, Tukoji. To serve people is to serve God. That's why I worked so hard to build roads for trade, keep taxes fair, and ensure justice for everyone.'

Tukoji's voice softened. 'Yes, you even had open court every day.'

Ahilyabai nodded. 'A ruler must be accessible. How can one lead without understanding the struggles of their people?'

Tukoji smiled. 'You built trust and hope, Your Highness.'

Ahilyabai's eyes shone with pride. 'That, Tukoji, is the greatest temple of all—a kingdom where people feel cared for. My devotion was not only to God but also to my people. That was my purpose as a ruler.'

A Queen's True Legacy

The setting sun cast a golden glow over Maheshwar Fort. Tukoji broke the silence. 'Your Highness, now I understand why people love you so much. You didn't just rule—you cared for them like a mother cares for her children.'

Schools Are for Girls Too!

At a time when girls rarely went to school, Ahilyabai Holkar encouraged their education. She believed that educated women could build a better society. She made sure women had access to learning and financial help to develop skills and crafts.

Ahilyabai smiled softly. 'A ruler must see their people as their children. Just as a mother's love is unconditional, so must a ruler's care. My joy was never in power or riches, but in seeing my people live in peace and prosperity.'

Tukoji nodded. 'The temples, roads, and wells you built, the justice you delivered—all of it shows your love for your people. Your reign has left a mark that cannot be erased.'

Ahilyabai's voice was gentle but firm. 'But my true legacy is not in the temples or the records of my rule. It is in the hearts of the people I serve. If they remember me as someone who cared for them, listened to them, and dedicated her life to their well-being, then I have done my duty.'

Tukoji's voice was strong. 'They do remember, Your Highness. And even centuries from now, your name will inspire devotion and respect. You have not just ruled a kingdom—you have ruled our hearts.'

Ahilyabai's smile deepened as she looked at him. 'And that, Tukoji, is enough for me.'

Learn More About Ahilyabai Holkar

'Your Highness, your life is an inspiration. But how will future generations learn about your legacy?'

'Our legacy is not just in memory but in the structures and records we leave behind. These will speak for us.'

- *Official Records and Inscriptions:* The Holkar dynasty's official documents in Indore detail administrative reforms, temple restorations, and infrastructure projects. Inscriptions on temples and public works mark my contributions.
- *The Kashi Vishwanath Temple Records:* These archives document my role in rebuilding the temple and preserving its spiritual and cultural significance for India.
- *Indore State Archives:* Records of our governance, tax policies, and justice systems provide insights into our administration.
- *Architectural Marvels:* Temples, ghats, wells, and rest houses, including Maheshwar Fort and the Ganga Ghat at Haridwar, stand as living testimonies to my vision. Historians and archaeologists continue to study these sites to understand our era.

- *Contemporary Accounts:* Scholars like Pandit Gangadhar Shastri wrote about my rule. Their writings offer glimpses of how our governance was perceived during my lifetime.
- *British Records:* Even the British East India Company acknowledged the stability and prosperity of the Holkar kingdom in their reports.

Uncover Hidden Histories

History is recorded in many ways—not just in books but also in buildings, stories, and even old letters. Look around your own surroundings:

- Are there any old temples, wells, or historical sites near you? Do you know who built them or why?
- Ask your parents or teachers if they have heard stories about how your town or neighbourhood has changed over time.
- Visit a museum or search online for historical records from your city. What do they tell you about the past?

At the same time, history is also about people's experiences. Like Ahilyabai, many around you have faced challenges with strength. Talk to a friend, family member, or someone who works in your home or school. Ask them:

- What was a difficult time they faced, and how did they overcome it?
- What did they learn from the experience?

Just like Ahilyabai's legacy lives on in records and monuments, every place and person has a story waiting to be discovered!

Community Builder Project

Materials needed: Paper, colouring supplies

Ahilyabai built temples, wells, and roads to help her people. Design your ideal community.

- Draw a map of a village or town.
- Include important buildings—schools, temples, wells, and hospitals.
- Mark where roads, bridges, and parks would be.
- Label each place and explain why it is important.

Share with your parents what you would build first if you were a ruler like Ahilyabai and why.

Royal Problem Solver

Materials needed: Paper, pen

Ahilyabai was known for listening to her people's problems and solving them fairly. Create a 'royal court' role-play.

- Have family members present different problems to the 'ruler'.

Example problems such as farmers need water for crops, two merchants argue over a shop location, and a village needs protection from bandits.

- The child plays the ruler who must listen carefully and make fair decisions.
- Parents can play advisors who offer suggestions.

Discuss afterward how difficult it is to make decisions that keep everyone happy, and what values help make good decisions.

Further Reading

- Pradeep Chakravarthy, *Leadership Shastra: Lessons from Indian History*, Penguin India, 2021.
- R.C. Majumdar, *The Holkars of Indore*, Bharatiya Vidya Bhavan, 1955.

- Vandana Bhandari, *Ahilyabai: The Great Queen*, Rupa Publications, 2016.
- Vikram Sampath, *Bravehearts of Bharat: Vignettes from Indian History*, Penguin India, 2022.

A royal seal from Ahilyabai Holkar's reign

Fun Quiz

Crossword 1

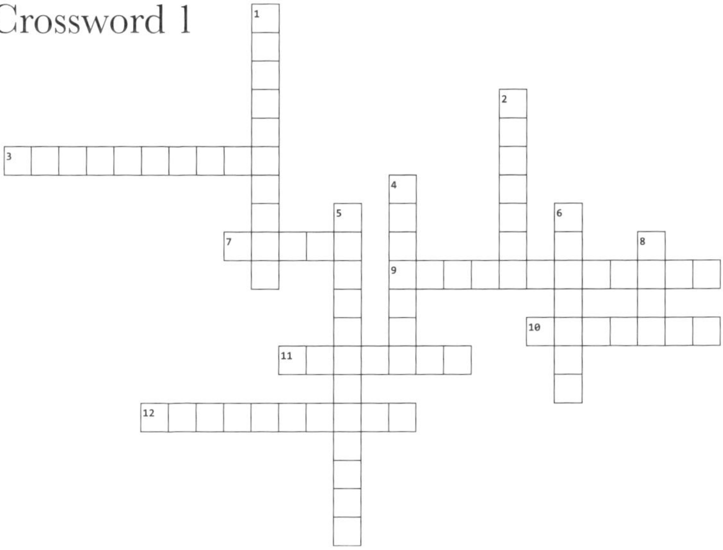

Across

3. Krishnadevaraya's witty court jester (10)
7. The temple in Varanasi restored by Ahilyabai (5)
9. Shivaji's council of eight ministers (12)
10. The river valley where Lalitaditya Muktapida's kingdom was located (7)
11. The building featured on the fifty rupee note from Krishnadevaraya's era (7)
12. What Lachit Borphukan said was more important than his uncle (10)

Down

1. The king of Kanauj defeated by Lalitaditya (9)
2. The fort captured by Tanaji Malusare for Shivaji with his ultimate sacrifice (7)
4. Shivaji's mother who influenced his character (8)
5. The empire ruled by Krishnadevaraya (11)
6. The river that gave peace to Ahilyabai at her fort in Maheshwar (7)
8. The kingdom Lachit Borphukan defended (4)

Answers

Across	Down
3. TENALIRAMA	1. YASOVARMAN
7. KASHI	2. KONDANA
9.ASHTAPRADHAN	4. JIJABAI
10. KASHMIR	5. VIJAYANAGARA
11. CHARIOT	6. NARMADA
12. MOTHERLAND	8. AHOM

Crossword 2

Across

3. Krishnadevaraya's witty court jester (10)
6. The fort that Krishnadevaraya captured which was considered 'unbreakable' (9)
7. The battle considered Lachit Borphukan's greatest victory (9)
9. The hidden weapon Shivaji used against Afzal Khan (8)
10. The concept of self-rule championed by Shivaji (6)
12. The region ruled by Ahilyabai Holkar (5)
13. Ahilyabai's trusted general mentioned in the chapter (6)

Down

1. Lalitaditya's most iconic temple creation (7)
2. The position Lachit was appointed to by King Chakradhwaj Singha (9)
3. The dynasty to which Lalitaditya Muktapida belonged (7)
4. The river that was crucial in Lachit Borphukan's victory against the Mughals (11)
5. The Telugu work written by Krishnadevaraya (13)
8. The Sanskrit chronicle that described Lalitaditya's life (12)
11. The dynasty Ahilyabai belonged to (6)

Answers

Across	Down
6. KONDAVIDU	1. MARTAND
7. SARAIGHAT	2. BORPHUKAN
9. WAGHNAKH	3. KARKOTA
10. SWARAJ	4. BRAHMAPUTRA
12. MALWA	5. AMUKTAMALYADA
13. TUKOJI	8. RAJATARANGINI
	11. HOLKAR

About the Author

Dr Pradeep Chakravarthy is a historian, author, and behavioural consultant with a passion for making history relevant to modern life. A graduate of the London School of Economics and Jawaharlal Nehru University, he holds a PhD on the role of temples in the socioeconomic and political life of medieval Tamil Nadu.

With over two decades of experience in learning and development, Pradeep has worked with leading organizations such as TVS, Cognizant, Infosys, and

McKinsey, using historical insights to drive behavioural change in individuals and businesses. His mission is to help people understand present and future behaviour by learning from the past.

He has authored 10 books focused on Tamil Nadu's rich cultural heritage and how historical wisdom can enhance workplace performance. His work has been featured in over 200 magazine and newspaper articles, and he has appeared as an expert on platforms such as Netflix (*Raja Rasoi*), History TV, Discovery Channel, and TEDx.

Most recently, he founded *Anantya in the Village*, a heritage hotel in Alwar Tirunagari, where he conducts immersive heritage tours for children, bringing history to life through experiential learning.